POMPEII

Sarah Blackmore

Published in association with The Basic Skills Agency

Hodder & Stoughton

A MEMBER OF THE HODDER HEADLINE GROUP

Acknowledgements

Cover: Stuart William

Photos: pp 3, 5, 20, 25 Hulton Getty; pp 10, 13, 17, 23 Mary Evans Picture Library

Every effort has been made to trace copyright holders of material reproduced in this book. Any rights not acknowledged will be acknowledged in subsequent printings if notice is given to the publisher.

Orders; please contact Bookpoint Ltd, 39 Milton Park, Abingdon, Oxon OX14 4TD. Telephone: (44) 01235 400414, Fax: (44) 01235 400454. Lines are open from 9.00–6.00, Monday to Saturday, with a 24 hour message answering service.
Email address: orders@bookpoint.co.uk

British Library Cataloguing in Publication Data
A catalogue record for this title is available from the British Library

ISBN 0 340 77641 2

First published 2000
Impression number   10 9 8 7 6 5 4 3 2 1
Year   2005 2004 2003 2002 2001 2000

Copyright © 1999 NTC/Contemporary Publishing Group, Inc.

Adapted for the Livewire series by Sarah Blackmore

Typeset by GreenGate Publishing Services, Tonbridge, Kent.
Printed in Great Britain for Hodder and Stoughton Educational, a division of Hodder Headline Plc, 338 Euston Road, London NW1 3BH, by Redwood Books, Trowbridge, Wilts

Where do you live?
Is it a town, a city or a village?
Are there lots of people?

It may be a busy place.
It may be a quiet place.
But each day people get on with their lives.
Doing things that they usually do.

What if something stopped that?
Something so terrible that it changed the place
for ever.

One day you hear a sound.
A deep, rumbling sound.
Maybe the earth trembles.
Is it an earthquake?

Then there is a bang.
An explosion.
Is it a bomb?

A large, black cloud hangs in the sky.
It is so big that it blocks out the sun.
Is it an eclipse?

An artist's drawing of the eruption of Mount Vesuvius
in AD 79.

It begins to rain.
Is it a thunderstorm?
But it's not rain.
It's hot pieces of rock.
It's hot pieces of stone.

It is a volcano.
A volcano has erupted.

Pieces of hot rock and stone rain down on the city.

What would you do?
You would need to protect yourself.
You would need to protect yourself from the falling stones.

Maybe you would hide under something.
Maybe you would tie a pillow on your head.
Maybe you would try to run away.
Maybe you would stay in your house.

This is what happened to a city.
It was a Roman city.
It was called Pompeii.

The city was built on the slope of a mountain.
The mountain is called Mount Vesuvius.
But it is not just a mountain.
It is a volcano.

For many years the volcano had been safe.
That's why Pompeii was built there.
Then one day the volcano exploded.

A black cloud formed over Mount Vesuvius.
It was shaped like a pine tree.
It blocked out the sun.

For seven days the volcano threw out ash and stone.
It also sent out gas.
Clouds of poisonous gas.
A gas called carbon monoxide.
This gas has no smell so people did not know
it was there.
It was so deadly that people died where they stood.

The eruption of the volcano which destroyed Herculaneum and Pompeii. Engraving after Hector le Roux.

The clouds of ash caused thunderstorms.
The rain mixed with ash and mud.
This mixture of volcanic ash and mud made a
type of paste.
A heavy paste.

This paste covered everything.
The whole city
and everybody in it.

A man stood by the city wall.
He was a soldier on guard.
Ash and stones fell down on him.
He stayed where he was.

He could not smell the gas.
It was poisonous but it had no smell.
It killed him.

At the same time he was covered in the paste.
He did not even fall over.

A man was in his house.
He was a rich man.
He had a pile of gold and silver.

He grabbed his sword.
He used the sword to stop other men from taking
his treasure.
He killed five men.
Then the gas reached him.
His body was covered in paste.
He was still holding his sword.

Some people tried to run away.
They tied pillows to their heads so that the stones
would not hit them.
Some were able to get away.
Others were struck down.
They were covered in paste.
It covered the pillows on their heads.

The paste covered people's houses.
It covered food on the table.
It covered bread baking in the oven.

It covered jugs of wine and bowls of fruit.
It covered tables, chairs and other furniture.
It covered paintings on the walls.
It covered people.

Excavating a wine bar. Nothing was broken, just covered in a thick paste.

As the paste cooled, it became hard.
In time it was covered by soil.
Plants started to grow.
The city of Pompeii was buried.

The city lay buried for nearly 2,000 years.
In 1748 it was uncovered.
People thought that there was hidden treasure.
They could not believe what they found.

The ruins of Pompeii today.

They uncovered the layers of soil with great care.
They uncovered the layer of hard paste with great care.

They found the food on tables.
They found jugs filled with wine.
They found fruit.
They even found olives in oil.
They could still be eaten.

They found bodies in the streets.
Some had pillows tied to their heads.

They found a man with a sword in his hand.
His foot was on a pile of gold and silver.
There were five other bodies near him.

They even found a Roman soldier.
He was still standing up.

The bodies of some of the victims of the eruption.

You can see the city of Pompeii today.
People from all over the world visit it.
They go to see the remains of the city.
About 700 bodies can still be seen.

The ruins of the House of Holconius in Pompeii.

700 bodies of people who lived in the city.
People who lived about 2,000 years ago.
People getting on with their lives.
Doing their usual things.
Until one day something happened.
Something that changed things for ever.